DEADLY BITERS

NILE CROCODILES BITE!

BY JANEY LEVY

Gareth Stevens
PUBLISHING

Please visit our website, www.garethstevens.com. For a free color catalog of all our high-quality books, call toll free 1-800-542-2595 or fax 1-877-542-2596.

Cataloging-in-Publication Data

Names: Levy, Janey.
Title: Nile crocodiles bite! / Janey Levy.
Description: New York : Gareth Stevens Publishing, 2021. | Series: Deadly biters | Includes glossary and index.
Identifiers: ISBN 9781538257784 (pbk.) | ISBN 9781538257807 (library bound) | ISBN 9781538257791 (6 pack)
Subjects: LCSH: Crocodiles--Juvenile literature. | Nile crocodile--Juvenile literature.
Classification: LCC QL666.C925 L48 2021 | DDC 597.98'2--dc23

First Edition

Published in 2021 by
Gareth Stevens Publishing
111 East 14th Street, Suite 349
New York, NY 10003

Copyright © 2021 Gareth Stevens Publishing

Designer: Reann Nye
Editor: Meta Manchester

Photo credits: Cover, p. 1 MariusLtu/iStock/Getty Images; cover, pp. 1-24 (background) Reinhold Leitner/Shutterstock.com; p. 5 Julian W/Shutterstock.com; p. 6 seaskylab/Shutterstock.com; p. 7 Peter Hermes Furian/Shutterstock.com; p. 8 Sanit Fuangnakhon/Shutterstock.com; p. 9 Shumba138/iStock/Getty Images; p. 11 Roger de la Harpe/Shutterstock.com; p. 12 Catchlight Lens/Shutterstock.com; p. 13 Jonathan Oberholster/Shutterstock.com; p. 15 muhd fuad abd rahim/Shutterstock.com; p. 16 Mari Swanepoel/Shutterstock.com; p. 17 Johan Swanepoel/Shutterstock.com; p. 19 PACO COMO/Shutterstock.com; p. 20 Daniel Hernanz Ramos/Moment/Getty Images; p. 21 florentina georgescu photography/Moment/Getty Images.

Printed in the United States of America

Some of the images in this book illustrate individuals who are models. The depictions do not imply actual situations or events.

CPSIA compliance information: Batch #CS20GS: For further information contact Gareth Stevens, New York, New York at 1-800-542-2595.

Find us on 🅕 🅞

CONTENTS

Words in the glossary appear in **bold** type
the first time they are used in the text.

NIFTY NILE CROCODILES

You've likely seen pictures of crocodiles, and maybe you've seen a real one at a zoo. But did you know about 14 species, or kinds, of crocodiles exist? Some are small and weigh as little as 13 pounds (6 kg). Others are huge. The Nile crocodile is one of the biggest. But size is only part of its claim to fame.

The Nile crocodile has the strongest bite of any animal alive today! Inside this book, you'll discover lots more about this crocodile and its bite.

CHEW ON THIS!

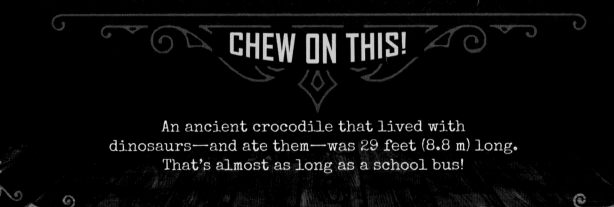

An ancient crocodile that lived with dinosaurs—and ate them—was 29 feet (8.8 m) long. That's almost as long as a school bus!

Nile crocodiles are also known by other names in different languages, including *mamba*, *garwe*, *ngwenya*, and *olom*.

THE NILE CROCODILE'S NEIGHBORHOOD

If you want to see Nile crocodiles in the wild, you must travel to Africa. They're water animals, so you'll find them around water. Because of their name, it won't surprise you to learn that they're found in Egypt's Nile River. They're also found in rivers and lakes throughout Africa south of the Sahara.

Nile crocodiles prefer freshwater, or water that's not salty, but some live in coastal **estuaries**. They can also be found in freshwater **swamps** and **mangrove** swamps.

CHEW ON THIS!

Nile crocodiles are found in over 40 African countries.

WHERE NILE CROCODILES LIVE

AFRICA

NILE CROCODILE
TERRITORY

MADAGASCAR

In addition to being found throughout large parts of Africa,
Nile crocodiles are also found in the island country of
Madagascar, off the southeastern coast of Africa.

A BIG BODY

Nile crocodiles are BIG animals. They can reach 20 feet (6.1 m) long and weigh up to 1,650 pounds (748 kg). That's longer than the average pickup truck! However, they're usually about 16 feet (4.9 m) long and weigh about 500 pounds (227 kg).

Nile crocodiles have a gray-green body with a yellowish stomach and a long, strong tail. Their front feet have five toes, which is usual for **reptiles**. The four toes on their back feet are **webbed**, which helps them swim.

CHEW ON THIS!

Nile crocodiles have long, strong **jaws**.

Male Nile crocodiles are larger than females.

SPECIAL FEATURES

Nile crocodiles have some amazing special features that help them survive. For example, they have salt **glands** on their tongue that get rid of extra salt. Because of these glands, Nile crocodiles can live in places like estuaries, which have salty water.

Perhaps most surprising, the crocodiles have **organs** all over the scales in their skin that measure touch, heat, cold, and **chemicals**. The organs help them catch **prey**, keep their bodies at the right temperature, and find good places to live.

CHEW ON THIS!

How do Nile crocodiles avoid swallowing water when they open their mouth to grab prey in the water? The secret lies in a special body part at the back of their throat.

Can you see the small dark spots in the Nile crocodile's skin?
Those are the special organs that measure
touch, heat, cold, and chemicals.

CARING CROCODILE PARENTS

Most reptiles lay their eggs and then leave. They don't stay to guard their eggs or care for their young. Nile crocodiles are different. The female digs a nest along a river and lays her eggs there. She guards them until they're ready to **hatch**.

Both parents gently roll the eggs in their mouths to break them slightly to help the babies come out. The mother then carries the young to water. The young stay in groups and older crocodiles care for them for up to two years.

CHEW ON THIS!

A female may lay up to 80 eggs! But even though she guards them, some get eaten by other animals when she has to leave to cool off in the water.

The female spends about three months guarding her nest!

A BEASTLY BITE

The Nile crocodile's powerful jaws hold 64 to 68 cone-shaped teeth. That's a lot! An adult human only has 32. Those sharp, pointed teeth can do lots of harm. But it's not just the teeth that make the Nile crocodile's bite deadly.

Nile crocodiles bite down with amazing force: 5,000 pounds per square inch, or psi (351.5 kg per sq cm)! How does that compare to you? Humans can only bite with a force of about 100 psi (7 kg per sq cm).

CHEW ON THIS!

While Nile crocodiles bite down with surprising force, they don't have much strength for opening their jaws. Their mouth can be held shut with just a rubber band!

Crocodiles lose teeth and grow new ones throughout their life. They may go through 8,000 teeth in their life!

TEETH

JAWS

ON THE HUNT

So what do Nile crocodiles eat? They're not using their sharp teeth and strong jaws to eat plants! These animals are carnivores, or meat eaters. Fish make up a lot of their meals. But they also eat zebras, giraffes, buffaloes, young hippos, birds, and large cats. They even eat other crocodiles!

Nile crocodiles are also happy to eat carrion, or dead, rotting animals. They're not really picky eaters. And they can eat up to half their body weight at a time!

CHEW ON THIS!

The average crocodile eats about 50 meals each year, but a large crocodile can go for over a year without eating!

Nile crocodiles kill their prey by drowning or squashing it. They swallow small prey whole. They shake and tear larger prey into pieces.

ARE YOU ON THE MENU?

Have you heard scary stories about crocodiles eating people? Do you wonder if these are true? It's not true for all kinds of crocodiles, but it *is* true for Nile crocodiles!

As you learned in the last chapter, Nile crocodiles aren't picky eaters. They'll eat just about anything. And a person in or near the water looks just as much like a meal as a giraffe or zebra does. So people in Africa do get eaten by Nile crocodiles!

CHEW ON THIS!

No one knows for sure, but it's believed Nile crocodiles kill as many as 200 people each year.

The Nile crocodile's eyes, ears, and nose are on top of its head, so it can hide under the water while it waits for prey to come close.

BEWARE THE NILE CROCODILE!

Nile crocodiles are some pretty amazing reptiles. Their size and their bite force set them apart from other crocodiles. So does the fact that they're such caring parents. Some people find Nile crocodiles so interesting they've tried to keep them as pets. But that's a bad idea.

Remember—these crocodiles are deadly predators that would just as happily eat you as they would eat a zebra. They belong in their wild homes. Respect Nile crocodiles—and don't get too close!

CHEW ON THIS!

Did you know a few Nile crocodiles have been found in Florida's swamps? They're likely pets that were dumped there or escaped.

Nile crocodiles can grow bigger, swim faster,
and jump higher than American crocodiles.

GLOSSARY

chemical: matter that can be mixed with other matter to cause changes

estuary: an area where the ocean's tide meets a river

gland: a body part that produces something needed for a bodily function

hatch: to break open or come out of

jaws: the bones that hold the teeth and make up the mouth

mangrove: a tree that grows in swamps or shallow salty water in warm parts of the world. It has roots that grow from its branches.

organ: a part inside an animal's body

prey: an animal that is hunted by other animals for food

reptile: an animal covered with scales or plates that breathes air, has a backbone, and lays eggs, such as a turtle, snake, lizard, or crocodile

swamp: an area with trees that is covered with water at least part of the time

webbed: connected by skin

FOR MORE INFORMATION

BOOKS

London, Martha. *Crocodiles*. Minnetonka, MN: Kaleidoscope, 2020.

Pope, Kristen. *On the Hunt with Crocodiles*. North Mankato, MN: The Child's World, 2016.

Schuetz, Kari. *Nile Crocodiles and Egyptian Plovers*. Minneapolis, MN: Bellwether Media, Inc., 2019.

WEBSITES

31 Facts About Africa's Nile Crocodile (*Crocodylus niloticus*)
uganda365.com/nile-crocodile/
Discover some fascinating facts about Nile crocodiles here, along with some great photos and a video.

How Strong Are a Nile Crocodile's Jaws?
www.wonderopolis.org/wonder/how-strong-are-a-crocodiles-jaws
Learn more about the amazing mouths of these fascinating predators.

Nile Crocodile
kids.nationalgeographic.com/animals/reptiles/nile-crocodile/
Check out this site for more fun facts and a map of where Nile crocodiles usually live.

INDEX